IN THE NAME OF

IN THE NAME OF

Love

GLADIS J. HALL

XULON PRESS

Xulon Press
2301 Lucien Way #415
Maitland, FL 32751
407.339.4217
www.xulonpress.com

Paperback ISBN-13: 978-1-66286-947-1
Ebook ISBN-13: 978-1-66286-948-8

This book is dedicated to my daughter, Sharon who has stood with me down through the years and encouraged me to be all that I can be in Christ. Supported and helped me when I needed it.

To co-pastor Bettye Dickens who encouraged me to write this book, that it might be a help to someone who is going through. Most importantly, to let people know that God is faithful and that he is a promise keep to all that love Him.

To Apostle Felix and First Lady Revills who I consider the greatest pastor and first lady ever lived.

To my sister Edrena who stuck with me and helped me through everything that I suffered and is still here helping and caring for me.

To my late sister Louvenia, who has passed and gone on with the Lord. This young lady truly loved me and was always there for me.

To my niece Ann who always come through for me and helped me when I was unable to do things for myself.

To all my church family who loves and support me in all my endeavors.

INTRODUCTION

This book "In the Name of Love" is a glimpse and summary of my life that shows the goodness, mercy and faithfulness of God. Many people who knew my story have said, "I don't see how you made it and how you survived all you went through, without giving up." Nevertheless, of all the things I went through, I kept the faith. There were many hardships, despair and atrocities, I suffered in my life, yet God was my refuge and my strength, my present help in trouble.

I hope this book encourage someone that you can still hold on to your salvation and serve God wholeheartedly when the enemy has put people in your life to sabotage your relationship with God. As my late founder, Apostle Isaiah Revills always said, "If you can take it, you can make it." God proved this saying to be so in my life. There is a quote in the bible that says, weeping may endure for a night but joy comes in the morning.

My encouragement to anyone reading this book, if you are suffering and in pain, stand in the faith of

God, knowing he will bring you through it. HE DID IT FOR ME!

Bishop Gladis Hall

CHAPTER ONE

B efore I formed thee in the belly, I knew thee and before thou camest forth out of the womb I sanctified thee, and I ordained thee a prophet unto the nations. (Jeremiah 1:5)

My life should have been a tragic one, but God turned my life from tragic to victory. When I look at the good, the bad, and the ugly that life dealt me, I praise God for His goodness and His mercy. Through my trials, heartache and pain, God made me an overcomer and not a victim.

I was born in Georgia in the small town of Colquitt in 1943. I am the sixth child of seven children, 2 brothers and 4 sisters.

As a child, I suffered from a spirit of rejection for I felt like the least among my siblings. I was always the one who got beat down and ridiculed.

When talking to one of my older sisters as an adult, she said, "but you were so mean". I don't recall being mean, but maybe I was.

When I was about seven or eight, I was arguing with my older sister, Joyce who was about fifteen, telling her

I would beat her and bounce her like a rubber ball. She was ironing at the time and she turned and stuck the hot iron to my arm. I still wear the mark on my arm today.

Growing up we lived in the big old wooden frame house that had fire places in each room. We didn't have sofas chairs back then, only rocking chairs, and cooked on an old wood burning stove.

My mother bought flour in 25-pound bags, with a flowered border. Mom made scarves for the chairs and dressers from these colorful flour sacks. My younger sister and I had our school clothes made from these same colorful flour sacks. We were a good match for the chair covers in the house. Our bras, panties and slips were made of a material called yellow muslin. Our brothers' shirts and under wear were made by our mother also.

I remember watching some of the girls at school in their store-bought clothes and wishing that I could have just one thing that come from the store, especially a bra and a slip with lace.

Fighting was nearly a daily occurrence in our home. If I wasn't fighting with my baby sister, who I will refer to as Audrey. I was fighting with my baby brother, Grady who was a year older than me. I was a very unhappy child. I was always heavy and when my siblings called me fat and ugly, that's how I felt. I would call my baby sister tar-baby by means of fighting back, because she was of a dark complexion.

My sisters and brothers seem to always protect her when we got into a fight and my brother would beat me up. I felt so alone.

Our mother was a beautiful woman with a compassionate heart and nature. Any one that had a need, or needed a place to stay was welcome in our home. When our neighbors needed food, mom was always giving whatever they needed. Those days was so different from today.

There was a stranger that came through our county and his car broke down and he didn't have any money. Some white people introduced him to my dad and he brought him home, and they let him stay with us for a week. When he left my mother fixed him sandwiches, bought him a few bars of Baby Ruth candy and gave him some spending money and sent him on his way.

When I was about ten years old, our mother mentally disabled older brother came to live with us. He was a gentle giant. He was more like an older brother than an uncle. He played with us, fought with us and baby sit us.

Once our uncle was at home with us and our baby brother started a fight and stabbed our uncle. When mom and dad came home there was blood everywhere. Mom and dad washed and cleaned the cuts and had to take him to the doctor for stiches. So back then we hardly ever went to doctors.

It seemed that we fought all the time. I remember when we were home alone our baby brother Grady would keep us in the house hours on end. He piled up bricks and rocks and every time we cracked open the door, he would throw a brick. My sister would open the door a crack to yell at him to stop and close the door quickly before he would throw his brick. One day after he and I started to fight, my older sisters shoved him out the door and hid me behind the bed. I raised my head to peep out just as they cracked the door and one of my brother's bricks hit me squarely in the eye. Even back then God was good to me and I didn't lose sight in my eye. All the whippings my brother got, it didn't stop him from throwing bricks when mom and dad was away. Broken bricks and rocks were all over the porch.

Our father was a farmer and worked for fifteen dollars per week. He took care of nine people with that amount of money. We didn't own a television at this time, really, I had never heard of a television, we only had radio.

Our father served as our part time entertainer when we weren't listening to the radio. Our father would play his guitar, sang to us, recite poetry and tell us stories about haints. We would be afraid to uncover our heads when we went to bed, regardless how hot it was.

We learned to sing and recite poetry at our father's knees. He knew more poems than any man that I have ever met, even to this day.

Even though my father had all these good qualities, he was also a week end drunk. When he was drunk, he was meaner than a snake and loved to fight. He was also a wife beater and a woman chaser.

CHAPTER TWO

My oldest sister married when I was about 10 years old and my mother sent my other sister to live with our aunt in New York and finish high school. She sent her there because our white boss had taken interest in her and our mom was determined that he was not going to touch her daughter. That left my two brothers, myself and my baby sister at home.

My father would come home on Friday or Saturday nights and jump on our mother. From Monday until Friday night we had a good father, but the weekend he was fighting and abusive. He would get his gun and chase us out of the house. Sometimes we would hide anywhere to get away from him, in the corn patch, behind the smoke house anywhere we could escape.

When I was still a young girl around thirteen, mom's young cousin moved into our home. She was about twenty-two years of age. My mother was trying to get her out of a sexual abusive relationship with her step-father. Little did mom know that she was bringing more trouble into an already bad situation.

After moving into our home, the young lady began having sexual relations with my father and my older brother. After learning that he wasn't the only one having sex with her my father became even more abusive. Our home became a war-zone. There was never any peace. The fighting increased. Father would jump on my older brother even when he was sober. My brother would never fight back, but try to hold him and keep him from hitting him. My baby brother didn't suffer any such problem. If dad hit him, he would lay him out, so dad never hit him. Finally, mom realized what was going on and put her cousin out of the house. The affair continued, but at least she was out of the house.

Somewhere in the mist of all this turmoil, our mother had a stroke. She became paralyzed on her left side and could not use her left arm and dragged her left leg. Since people hardly went to doctors, my mom was no exception. Mom was in bed for a long time talking out of her head.

Our older sister would come to help me and our baby sister care for her, even though she was being abused by her husband. He was fighting and beating her. He also was a woman chaser. She was also the mother of three boys.

When I was fourteen years old, my sister that had moved to New York had become a mother. She brought her five-month-old son, named Ronald, home to see mom. Even though mom was not able to fully take care of the child, she refused to allow my sister to take him back to New York with her.

Our baby sister was still at home but I bonded more with the baby and I became his mom at fourteen, for our mom gave me charge of the baby. I was still in school but had to get up with the baby during the night, fix bottles and change diapers. My baby sister was there to help but the baby became so attached to me that the minute I walked through the door from school, he didn't want anyone else but me.

I was a hard sleeper and sometime when the family would sit on the porch at night, I would fall asleep with the baby in my arms. Mom said they couldn't wake me so they would go inside the house and leave me and the baby on the porch. There were times when the baby would wake for some reason, and beat me in the face until I would wake and carry him inside. Mom would always warn me saying, "don't you sit there and go to sleep because you know that we can't wake you up". I never listened. I was told that sometime mom would whip me while I was asleep but I wouldn't wake, only the baby could wake me. I loved that little boy with all my heart and soul. Our father continued to be mean and abusive.

CHAPTER THREE

B oth of my brothers left home. One moved to New York and the other to Quincy City, Florida. Only my baby sister and I was left at home.

My older sister husband went to prison for a year for man slaughter. He was driving and drinking and had an accident where the passenger in the car with him was killed. My sister had to move back home with her children. Now she was there all the time when daddy wanted to fight and fight, we did. Every weekend we had to fight. Our baby sister would help us fight, but daddy would never hit her. He said, "that's my baby". I think the real reason was that she was so much like him in looks and in meanness.

One day he came home cursing and shoving and couldn't get my older sister to fight. Her small son was watching television. (Oh yes, we had finally got a black and white television). Daddy grabbed the child by the arm, lifted him up and started hitting him. He knew that would make my sister fight and she did. When she started to fight him, I jumped on him and started to help her. Our baby sister jumped in and started helping us. There we were all four of us tied up fighting. When I say fighting, our father would really hit us with his fist.

Mom could only sit there and plead with us to stop. She wasn't able to do anything else. One thing my father never did even when he was drinking, he never bothered my mother retarded brother. He always took up for him when he got in trouble.

Our father would come home after getting drunk on the weekend and start cursing one of us. If that didn't get him the fight that he wanted to start, then he would start shoving us. No matter how much we begged and pleaded it didn't do any good. We were cursed and called every bad name a person could be called.

My sister's husband came home from prison and she went back to her home with him and continued to have children.

CHAPTER FOUR

I met a young man in high school and started dating him. He was eight years my senior but he made me feel special. He seems to be the exact opposite of my father and brother-in-law and I needed someone gentle in my life, someone that made me feel loved.

I graduated high school a few months shy of my seventeenth birthday and started working for the same white couple that my sister husband worked for. Finally, I could have store bought clothes whenever I wanted. I bought my baby sister clothes and helped my older sister with her children when her husband didn't provide for them. I bought milk, shoes, and clothes for her boys.

My baby sister sneaked away and married at sixteen. I was so hurt when I found out that she had done this and so was our mother but she accepted it. They lived with us for a short while and then moved to New Jersey.

One Sunday night my father came home drunk, I was the only one at home and he started punching and shoving me. I tried getting out of his way but he followed me. I ran out the door with him right behind me. I remember that we had a clothe line on the side of the house that was barb wire. As I ran looking back to see how close he was on me. I ran into that barb wire. It picked me up and threw me flat on my back. When I came to myself and got up half of my right ear was almost ripped off from my head. When I came back inside the house my father was still cursing and trying to fight me.

When I look back now, one thing I hate more than the fighting was the fact that I would stand toe to toe with my father and curse him for all the bad names he cursed me for.

Sometime I would curse him until my voice would cut completely off and I couldn't make a sound, but I would still be trying to curse him.

Mother would try to stop me many times. She would call my name and say "that's your father" I would scream and tell her "I don't give **** who he is" and continue cursing him as he cursed me.

I don't remember any of my sisters or brothers cursing him as I did. They would curse but not directly at him, with the exception of my oldest brother and he wouldn't even do that.

The last fight I had with my father when he came home drunk was also on a Sunday. He started on me pushing, shoving and cursing me. I got out of his way by running around the kitchen table. He chased me round and round but as I ran, I picked up a knife that was lying on the table. Finally, he caught me grabbed me in the bosom and was about to hit me. Mom came up and tried to stop him. He had this sinister look on his face, a twisted half smile. He caught Mom by the arm that she couldn't move and twisted it, still with that sinister look. For as long as I live, I'll never forget my mother's screams. When she began screaming, I began screaming also but I was screaming "I'll kill you, I'll kill you". As I screamed those words at him, I was stabbing him with the knife. Before my mom could stop me, I had stabbed my dad seven times.

I know now that God had a plan for my life and it didn't include killing my father, because the knife that I had picked up wasn't a pointed knife even though I didn't know it at the time. Now it reminds me of the scripture, Jeremiah 29:11, "For I know the thoughts that I think toward you, saith the Lord, thoughts of peace and not of evil, to give you and expected end."

All the knife did was cut him up badly. He never went to the doctor, because mom was right there seeing about him, washing and tending to the cuts. No matter what he did, mom was always there for him. I couldn't understand how she treated him so good when he treated her so bad because, then, I would have let him die and said good riddance. Today, I thank God for a new mind.

My only outlet was going out with my friends and dancing. I loved to dance. The young man I was dating would pick me and my friends up on Saturday night and go clubbing. This way I wasn't home on Saturday night and could avoid my father at least until Sunday night because no matter when he came home it was a fight.

I loved those times and felt good when I got on the dance floor. The attention I got when I was dancing made me feel good. That was the place where I was free and without worries.

I worried about my mom and how violent my father was. I wanted her out of the house and away from him. My father had stopped fighting her, but she was always there trying to stop him from fighting us. I would call her sister in New York beg her to send at my mother, but she never did. Little did I know that she had an affair with my father and had a child with him. So, she thought he was all that, and a bag of chips. I found this out only after my mother died.

CHAPTER FIVE

F our months after my nineteenth birthday, I married the man that I met and dated since I was sixteen and finally, I was out of the house away from my father and it was great. My husband seemed to love me. He made me feel like somebody; I was happy. My husband lived with his father in a small town called Newton. They owned a farm and that is where he took me. His father was cripple and walked with crutches. When I came to their home, I started helping with him. Looking back now, I have to smile because he never got my name right even though I lived with him more than three years before he died.

His daughter lived next door on the same farm. Some of my husband sister's children were the same age as my husband but I thought we could still have a good relationship. She always referred to me as her brother's little wife. Little did I know the misery, the pain and the heartache that one lady would cause me. My husband was twenty-seven years old; I was nineteen and her oldest son was twenty-seven so she had to be in her late forties or early fifty's.

From the first she seemed to resent me. She was the mother of eight children, but only three still lived at home. The ones at home were two boys and one girl, ages from 14 to 17. Her oldest son and I became fast friends.

My husband's brother lived on the same farm but a short distance away; a father with two sons and four daughters.

The house that we lived in was the home house and the gathering place for the boys and their friends. The family boys had to come to help bathe and do for their grandfather. Some time they met and played games or played cards. The house was a very large house. Even though this was the gathering place before I came, my husband sister started telling family members and her friends that I was having sex with these boys. I remember how I would cry. I was in a strange place and didn't have friends and wasn't accustomed to people lying on me without reason.

Only her oldest son and her brother oldest daughter I could relate to. Her son would tell me, "Don't let her make you cry, you know it's not true." It still hurt because she was putting my name out as a bad person even telling my husband. She had a married boyfriend that she was keeping company with, but she made me the bad person. It looked like I had traded one hell for another, only a different kind. This was only the beginning of the atrocities that she did against me.

I married in 1962 and in 1963, my mom gave me the little boy that I had help raised. He was turning six and mom couldn't get him ready for school. This only made my sister-in-law even more angry. Now her brother had to take care of someone else child. My husband didn't mistreat the little boy, but all his sister's fussing didn't make it easy. He told his sister, "If that is what she wants, she can have it", but he never bonded with my son.

From the first time I brought my son home, my sister-in-law baby son took pleasure in hurting him. He was fifteen now and never hit my son, but found ways to torment him. My son was the only thing that I would fight for and many times nearly came to blows with him. There were no small children for my son to play with, so when I let him go outside to play this young man would throw stones at him, scare him and keep him crying. Here was another battle I had to fight. I loved my son and couldn't see giving him up.

My mom died the next year in January of 1964, and my father-in-law at the end of the same year. My son's real mom would have taken him gladly but she had two other children by now and my father said no she couldn't have him, I was over joyed.

CHAPTER SIX

I n April 1966, a gospel tent came to our small town. Many people flocked to the tent. This gospel tent was the talk of the town. People were talking about being saved and filled with something called the Holy Ghost.

People were dancing, shouting, falling out and rolling in the dirt when this man laid hands on them. I thought it was the worst thing in the world, this man fooling all these people. People that I knew was shouting and acting like they were crazy. Then one night my husband wanted to go and see the happenings. Was it really true what the people were saying?

My first experience after reaching the gospel tent was the great singing and the beautiful music. People were dancing, shouting and having a good time, and I began to enjoy myself. When the elder called the prayer line, I was standing at the back of the tent. He called out to me and said, "You little girl in the pink dress (I was wearing pink at that time) God says to get in the line." When the man of God laid hands on me, something changed in me. I had never felt like that before in my life. Unfortunately, when I came through the line, my husband was waiting on me. The prayer workers were trying to help me, but my husband grabbed me and said, "Let's Go!"

I never had the chance to go to the tent again, but for the next few weeks, I found myself praying and reading the bible. There was a peace that come into my life, but it eventually vanished and I was back to the old me.

Things continued to function as usual, me trying to please my sister-in-law and she still criticizing me to her friends and acquaintances. This woman seemed to have every intention of destroying me while wearing a smile and saying she was a Christian.

Her oldest son, who was my friend left home and joined the Navy. Then after a few years, he returned home. His mom didn't skip a beat, now my husband told her son that he couldn't come to the house except when he was home. He was beginning to listen to his sister.

Finally, her son met and married a young lady from another small town called Arlington. I was so happy now. I had a friend; someone I could share with.

I was still friends with my brother-in law daughter but didn't see much of her because she was in college. I was overjoyed to have another friend called Ann. My sister-in-law didn't want me to get close to her daughter-in-law so she told her that I had slept with her husband. This young lady was and still one of the bravest people that I had ever met. She didn't beat around the bush but came directly to me. Somehow, she saw beyond her mother-in-law lies and saw the truth. She would stand up to her mother-in-law and tell her what she wanted her to know. My sister-in-law began to resent her daughter-in-law, but couldn't do anything with her. This girl even threatened to hit her mother-in-law if she didn't stay out of her business.

Even this didn't stop my sister-in-law from trying to put a wedge between us. My brother-in-law's daughter, Laverne was home so my sister-in-law started telling her daughter-in-law Ann, we were not her friends, that we were talking against her, but she came directly to us and that lie fell through and we remained friends.

My brother-in-law's daughter, Laverne became pregnant and left town, because she said I know she is going to drag my name through the dirt, so she only told me and my oldest sister Joyce since she wasn't married. She would have the baby in Chicago and put it up for adoption and no one here would ever know. My sister-in-law did find out because Lavern's brother lived in Chicago and my sister-in-law oldest son lived there too.

This woman talked about this girl to anyone who would listen. She made sure her mother knew also. Lavern's mom was a school teacher and I believed she resented her also. My friend had no other choice but to bring her baby home for she had a teaching position waiting on her that same month in Moultrie Georgia.

TRULY MY SISTER-IN-LAW WAS AN EVIL VINDICTIVE WOMAN!

CHAPTER SEVEN

In August 1966, God gave me the greatest gift that could be given. He gave me a baby daughter. I was so happy for when they laid that baby in my arms my life was complete. I had two children, now a boy and a girl. My son was about nine years old at this time.

My sister-in-law's son lived in a trailer nearly in my yard and his mother lived on the other side of him. We were all in talking distance from each other. I could stand on my porch and talk to his wife at her trailer and if I raised my voice I could talk to my sister-in-law. We lived that close.

My friend Ann started working at Newton Manufacturing company making women's undergarments. After working there for a while, she convinced me to start working there. The company worked two shifts and I started on the night shift. Before working my first night, Ann had left for another job in Albany.

I worked hard at my job and less than a year I was transferred to the day shift. The only blacks that worked on this shift were the males that fixed the machines. After about another three or four months, they brought other black women to the day shift.

One of these young ladies, I knew from my home town. She had another older lady that she would be with. Immediately, I started talking to them at break and invited them to ride with me for lunch. I was so glad to have someone to talk to and not be alone.

I soon discovered that there was something different about these ladies. The only thing they wanted to talk about was Jesus. It was Jesus this and Jesus that, no matter what I tried to talk about they found some way to get it back to Jesus. The youngest of the ladies, namely the one from my home town, when she talked, she would start bouncing in the back seat from excitement. All I wanted to do was slap her upside the head and tell them to get out of my car, but of course, I didn't. I was so sick of hearing about Jesus, Jesus, Jesus. After inviting them to ride with me, I didn't know how to stop them, so every day they headed to my car since both of them caught rides to work. I would go home and complain to my husband that I was sick and tired of them.

Then one day I started to listen to them. I would sit quietly and listen at how much God seem to mean to them. This was their whole conversation at break and at lunch time. It was always what a great time they had in church, how God moved and how people were healed and delivered.

Years before after coming to Newton, I would pray that God would give me a God-fearing family. At the time, I was just thinking that what I wanted would be a good family that went to church regularly. I didn't know the depth of what I was asking.

Listening to these two ladies, I started wanting God to mean as much to me as he did to them. At the time, I was a smoker, and had been smoking since I was thirteen years old.

Sitting in that car listening to them something had happened to me, now I wanted what they had. So, one day I said "I'm going to stop smoking." The older lady looked at me, smiled and said, "That's good but you need to do it all, and get the Holy Ghost."

All the time they were with me they never criticized me even though I smoked and sometime cursed then would look at me and continue their Jesus conversation. They never pressured me to do anything, not even come to church.

Finally, I talked my husband into taking me to the church that was in Newton. I was amazed. The people were singing, shouting, clapping hands, dancing, no one sitting down. I felt a presence that I had only once before experienced and that was under the gospel tent six years earlier.

The pastor was an Elder and when he laid hands on me my heart felt so full it was nearly busting. That Thursday night I received the Holy Ghost. For once my husband just watched. He later said that he never thought I would join that church, which I didn't that night but the next Thursday night, I became a member of that church. I was so excited telling everyone that I was saved and all hell broke loosed in my life.

My sister-in-law, if I thought she was against me before, it was nothing like she came against me then.

CHAPTER EIGHT

My husband's mother died when he was about eight years old, and even though she was his sister, she was also the mother figure in his life.

From the moment, I professed that I was Holy Ghost filled, she seemed to double her efforts to turn my husband against me. She would tell my husband, "Your little wife is at that church, and at certain times they turn the lights off and she has to wrap up in a sheet with one of the men, and roll in the dark. Talk about being sanctified, she is not even satisfied. She is nothing but a liar and a cheat, she's cheating on you, She ain't nothing." This was always her message to him.

I tried and tried to tell him differently, but never could get him to completely believe me. My husband always drank beer, but he was never a drunkard, but he began to drink heavy. He would sneak around the church when I was there peeping in to see what I was doing, he even confessed to crawling under the church to listen. (Our church at that time sit high off the ground).

One night he was drunk and came to the church, I was sitting on the front seat, he came in screaming and cursing, calling my name saying, "bring your ***out of there and let's go home. Of course, the deacon rushed and got to him before he got to me, trying to restrain him, pulling him out still cursing and screaming. I had to go out to help with him and take him home.

Even in this I stayed as faithful as I could. Many times, I had to cry and beg in order to go to church. Another lady had gotten save a few months after I did and she would help me beg to be able to go to church. Her name was Edrena.

As time passed, the wedge that my sister-in-law was planting seemed to grow even wider. My husband worked at a place called Merck's Refrigeration Company in Albany, Georgia. He would go to work every day from Monday until Friday. When Friday came a fear would grip me, if he wasn't home by six o'clock in the evening. The later it became the more nervous I became. If he wasn't home by seven, I would start screaming and crying because I knew he wasn't coming and when I did see him, he would be completely broke. Every weekend he would stay after work drinking and gambling with his friends.

Many nights after putting my children to bed, I would go walking trying to find him. We didn't have a telephone at that time but his brother did so I would get on the phone and call everyone that I knew trying to see if someone had seen him.

This went on for weeks his gambling and drinking and spending his whole check. Finally, it came to a point where I couldn't feed me and the children. I was working at the factory but my check couldn't pay all the household bills and my husband had traded our car that was paid for and got a newer more expensive car. We didn't have but this one car and my husband would become violent, cursing and screaming if the payments on the car wasn't paid. I never told anyone that I didn't have enough food in the house, not even my church family. I was so ashamed. My sister-in-law saw what I was going through and knew the problems I was having. She made the statement that she would help me if I gave up my children and that I could never do. I learned in my going through that God is a provider. Psalm 37:25, David said, "I have been young and now am old, yet I have not seen the righteousness forsaken, nor his seed begging bread."

There was an Overseer/Mother in our church that God always sent when I needed food the most. She would ask, "do you get commodity" and I would say, "no" and she would say, "I have this canned meat and these dry noodles, that my children won't eat, do you want them?" Other times she would say, "my husband went fishing and caught all these carb fish and I've got so many, do you want some of them." This is how I fed my family. I would boil the noodles and pour the canned meat over them or cook the fish, pull all the bones out and that's what we would eat.

My sister in Christ, Edrena, lived about a half mile from me and we were good friends. She was having problems with her husband also because she was saved.

We cried on each other shoulder, or at least I cried because she was the kind of person that wouldn't take a whole lot and would fight if you pushed her. Often times we went to her house and she would feed us. I cried so much and it came to a point where I thought I just couldn't take anymore. I couldn't feel anything but the pain that was in my heart. I was so burdened that I began to think that death is better than this. Sometimes when I was driving the car, the enemy would say to me, "All you have to do is just run into that light pole and end it all and you wouldn't have to go through all of this." I think now that God always allowed me to have my little girl in the car with me and I knew I could never do that to her. God saved my life through my little girl.

CHAPTER NINE

My husband had spent a year in Milledgeville Institution before I met him and my sister-in-law preyed on that. She would make up lies to tell him to make him mistrust me and finally my husband cracked under the pressure. He had to be put in Southwestern State Hospital for the mental disable.

She lied on me until I was ashamed to go down town. When I would walk by all the men would stop what they were doing, fold their arms and just stare at me as if I was dirt.

One night alone, in my bed I was crying and feeling this terrible pain in my heart and I felt a presence come to my bed, I felt the bed give way as it sat. Something took me in its arms and just held me. I wasn't afraid and stopped crying and just lay there in the comfort of who-ever or whatever it was that held me. I will always believe that it was Jesus comforting me.

In 1975, a preacher from Africa came to the church in Albany and our leader had him preach in a revival. I remember not wanting to go to church, but I was always faithful, and others were depending on me as a way to get to church. When we got there the music was playing and everyone were singing and dancing having a good time. I was still unable to feel anything but pain, and didn't want to go inside because I was hurting so bad. I went to the kitchen to avoid going inside. I had told myself this is it; I can't face another day. When I got to the kitchen one of the mothers from our church was there and she was so excited. She said, come on let's go inside they are having a good time. I wanted to make an excuse and tell her no, but she took me by the hand and started leading me inside.

When we came inside the church it was packed. People were standing up all over the church. I came through the double doors and stood with my back pressed against the door. The leader of the church was up and he was calling people out, prophesying and praying for them. They were falling out under the anointing. Then he turned toward the door that I had come through and said, "You in the red dress raise your hands." There were another lady standing there and she raised her hands. My dress was red with black, but he said to lady, "not you but the other one." Pointing at me he said, "God says that you are under a heavy burden, but God says he is going to release you from some of it." He prayed for me, he didn't touch me, but when he prayed, I felt something heavy fall off me and it fell around my feet. The pain in my heart left, immediately. I could feel something besides the pain. I could smile, I could laugh, I could dance. I never heard our leader pray for anyone else like that before, that God said he was going to release you from some of it. Hebrew 13:5, "Jesus said I will never leave you or forsaken you."

I still had to contend with my husband, sister-in-law and his brother who had started coming to the house cursing because I was holy, but God had equipped me that night. Now I could handle all the lies, the slander and the cursing that they were putting me through.

CHAPTER TEN

My husband's mind seemed to only function right about a couple of months and he would start back acting up and we would have to put him back in the hospital. He wouldn't take his medication because he said he didn't like the way they made him feel.

One time when my husband's mind went bad, he went missing for a week. We looked for him everywhere. Finally, we got word that he was locked up in Blakely, Georgia. The Sheriff in Blakely said they had finally got enough out of him to call the Sheriff in Newton. I had no idea how to get to Blakely because I had never been there before and was afraid. My sister-in-law told her son not to help me, but let me figure out how to get him myself. He was still my friend, him and his wife, Ann. He refused and told his mom there was no way that he wouldn't help me, that my husband was his uncle and her brother. He told me how bad it made him feel for his mom to say that.

He took me to Blakely and found my husband in jail. The sheriff in Blakely had become afraid of my husband because he was talking out of his head. He thought he was on his job laying pipes. Every time he laid an imaginary pipe, he would flush the commode. He had over run the cesspool and the cell was full of water. They were afraid to open the cell to feed him and he had lost a lot of weight.

When they took us to the cell the first thing he said was to his nephew, "oh you are not working today, hold on I've got to lay this pipe." He was talking to his other imaginary nephew saying, "oops hold it straight." Then he would flush the commode. We had to send for the sheriff in Newton to come and get him and take him back to the hospital in Thomasville. We knew that he was not going to listen to us and the Blakely sheriff said that they were going to turn him a loose to get rid of him.

For the next few years my husband was in and out of the hospital. But I remained faithful to him and to God and to the church.

CHAPTER ELEVEN

I don't remember the year we got a new pastor. Our first pastor was an elder from Moultrie, but this pastor lived in Newton. Our leader said because he lived in Newton, he should pastor Newton.

Now my troubles quadrupled even though I didn't know it at the time. We cried when out first pastor left and had to adjust to a new pastor. The people at church knew this pastor because he was a previous member before he became a pastor, and he helped many of them come to Christ.

God had elevated this pastor to be an Overseer and later an Apostle. This Apostle was a holy terror especially to me and the young people at Newton.

Our first pastor had appointed me assistant pastor to him after being called into the ministry for only one year. There were other ministers in the church, some older than me, but God chose me.

When Apostle came to Newton, he let some of the people know that he didn't want me as his assistant. He began looking to the other ministers to replace me, but everyone he chose couldn't handle the job that I was doing. I was accustomed to handling the bills, the people, working with them, helping with whatever problems they faced and they loved me.

Psalm 124:2-3 says, "If it had not been the Lord who was on our side, when men rose up against us, then they had swallowed us up quick, when their wrath was kindled against us."

For some reason the Apostle always praised me to the leader, he would say, "I don't know what I would do without her, she sees about everything." And that I did. I tried to keep everything off him. He never had to see about any of the business, but every opportunity he tried to hurt me in some way. One day he stood in the pulpit and said that one of the other ministers (namely Edrena) was better than me, I was nothing but a chicken. It was like a knife in my heart, I was so hurt.

He had to travel a lot, going to the outer churches and I was left at the church. He would instruct me in what to do, then call and tell the deacons not to obey me, that I wasn't over them that they were over me. He would tell the secretary not to tell me anything going on in the church, but he expected me to take care of everything at the church. I didn't know he was doing this until the secretary got tired of him doing this and told me for, she said that's not right.

I was so surprised, but she said, "Ask the deacons", which I did. When I asked one deacon he just said yes, he did. When I asked the chairman deacon, he really didn't want to tell me, but I insisted and he finally broke down and told me yes it was true. They didn't listen to him but still stood with me to help me accomplish whatever he had told me to do.

The Apostle also had a bad habit of slapping the young girls at church. One day we were to follow him to Blakely for night service after being in Newton all day. One of the young girls was sick and had a high fever. She was really sick and we all knew it. She was about fifteen at the time. I remember him calling her into his office, I went to the lady's restroom because I could hear him fussing at her through the wall. Then I heard the slap, I ran out of the restroom into the office just in time to keep her from hitting him. I screamed her name and told her to stop. She burst into tears and threw herself in my arms saying, "he didn't have to hit me like that. Apostle whole hand print was in her face. She was very light skinned and you could see the hand print was in her face. I ended up making her go to Blakely anyway.

Apostle didn't believe in any of us staying home for any reason. If someone in your family died you still had to go to church. Regardless of how he treated me or the young people, we loved him with all our hearts.

He didn't treat anyone else in the church as he treated us. There was another lady in the church he was hard on, but could only go so far with because her husband was in the church.

There was a time when I was sick, and was told my body was down. I didn't understand what that meant, only I couldn't stand up straight for the pain. He called me and I told him I was sick and couldn't stand up right and wouldn't be able to come to church. He got angry and told me to come to church anyway. I had to get out of bed, bent from the waist down for he said, "you don't have to do anything but sit there and I will pray for you." I got up went to church bent over holding my stomach. A few minutes before he came in from his office, he sent word to me to get ready I had to preach that day. I walked into that pulpit nearly in tears from pain, but God is faithful, a few minutes after I started ministering, the pain left and I was able to stand straight and preach.

There was another time, I was suffering with a migraine headache and had to shut up in a dark room to get relief. He told me I had to come to church, and when I got there in pain and the light hurt my head so badly that I had a problem keeping my eyes open, he told me I had to preach. He always made me preach when he knew I was sick. God taught me something, if I would make myself stand and preach regardless to how I felt, He (God) would always heal my body, as I preached.

In all of this, I never complained or talked against my pastor. I still stood and helped him in any way I could and never taught the members against him. I had every opportunity to do so, but I taught them to love him and stand with him.

He held me responsible if the members didn't have money and would call me fussing asking me what do I mean the people didn't have money. My sister, Edrena that lived a short distance from me and one of the senior deacons became my protectors.

My sister, Edrena would tell him, "She can't help it if I don't have money so don't call her." She would stand up to him, and he learned he couldn't treat her any way. Therefore, she got by with a lot, he would say, "she was crazy and didn't have good sense, but she was his baby."

One night while the Apostle was away and I was in charge of the church. A visitor came. Sister Edrena's daughter and one of the visitor's family members got in an argument. Sister Edrena got in the argument telling the girl if she hit her daughter what she would do to her. I tried to stop her because this girl's family was there and they weren't saved and was watching, but she wouldn't be stopped. When the Apostle came back to church, I told him what she had done. He called her in the office laughing. He tapped her on the shoulder and hugged her saying, "You are crazy, what am I going to do with you, you big baby." He did not chastise her or rebuke her only laughed with her. Many times, Sister Edrena would get angry at the Apostle and leave the church walking. I always had to catch her and convince her not to leave. She was mean spirited and determined to have her way, and the majority of the time she got it.

CHAPTER TWELVE

My husband's brother was a mean blood thirsty man that love to boss people, make them do what he wanted and if you refused, he would get his gun and threaten you. Since he was my baby's grandfather, he thought he could get drunk and come take her when he pleased. He was always threatening me with a gun or a knife. My daughter was so afraid of him, she would try to hide any place she could. One day he came to the house cursing and threatening and after he left, I looked for her, I found her between the bed mattress, trembling and shaking.

One day my brother-in-law came to the house drunk and told my daughter that he would kill her and she became hysterical, she was shaking so bad that she couldn't move or speak. She was jittery, jumping from fright. I had to start screaming at her calling her name shaking her to bring her out of it.

Here I was, my husband, my sister-in-law, my brother-in-law on one side and the Apostle on the other.

My life seemed to be on a roller coaster, up and down. I had to put my husband back in Southwestern Mental Hospital and he stayed for a month. I went to pick him up on a Wednesday. Saturday evening his brother came and asked him to take him to this club. I told him that my husband wasn't able to drive and anyway he didn't have license. He began cursing and saying, "He didn't care, that he still wanted him to take him.

Finally, my husband said, "just let me take him so he will hush and go home", so I said alright. My husband was only gone for about an hour and came home. He said to me, "I had to leave my brother because I told him I was feeling sick and had to go but he refused.

Sunday morning, my husband was cleaning up the car for me because I was going to church. His brother came behind him and I heard him say, "You left me yesterday, then he shot my husband in the back twice. My husband ran around the back of the house screaming, "He shot me, he shot me." He was calling my name as he screamed. I ran to the door and my brother-in-law was standing there reloading his gun, then I ran and got my husband's shotgun, ran to the door and shot over my brother-in-law's head to get him to leave so I could go see about my husband. When I did this, he turned and shot at me twice with my daughter standing in the door. The bullets lodged in the door frame where I was standing.

My brother-in-law shot my husband twice but had shot at him about four times for his other shots burst out the back and side windows of my car.

When I reached my husband, I thought his brother had only shot to scare him, but he told me to pull up his shirt and look. The amazing thing was, my husband wasn't bleeding at all, but when I lifted his shirt, there were two bullet holes in his back. I called the police but they didn't come, so I got my husband in the car along with my daughter and went to the police station. They told me that they had called the ambulance and it would meet me. My husband still wasn't bleeding but sitting and talking to me telling me how fast to drive.

We finally met the ambulance and they put my husband on the stretcher and he never said another word and blood began to pour from his body.

I believe God was protecting me, because if my husband had passed out and I saw a lot of blood, I would have panicked.

Psalm 86:15 says, "But thou oh Lord, are a God full of compassion and gracious, longsuffering and plenteous in mercy and truth."

I know that someone may say, that don't make sense. But one time before he shot my husband, he was trying to fight his wife. She ran and hid so he couldn't fine her, so he shot his baby daughter so his wife would come out of hiding. When his wife heard her daughter screaming "momma, momma, daddy has shot me" she ran from her hiding place and he stabbed her. The only reason he didn't shoot his wife was that they had hid his bullets and he had only one.

He calmly walked to my house and said, "You better go see about them, because I shot my daughter and stabbed my wife." Then he walked the few yards to his sister's house and had coffee with her. When I got to his wife's house, I found that he had done this thing, his wife and daughter was at the emergency room.

I believe the police in our town was a little afraid of him, for they didn't bother him. One day when he had done something the police came and he sat on his door step with his shot gun across his lap and dared them to get out of the car and they didn't.

My husband nearly died from the gun shots that he received. He was in intensive care for over a week and I stayed with him night and day. After a few weeks at the hospital, he finally came home. Now my husband had something else to deal with. I was still working and my husband wasn't able to see about himself. I had to ask my sister-in-law for her help.

CHAPTER THIRTEEN

One day my sister Edrena's husband fell off a truck loader and she couldn't find anyone to drive her to the hospital. So, she called me from the job to take her. My sister-in-law got so angry at me that she refused to help me out with my husband (her brother) in any manner.

I had asked her to warm my husband food at lunch time, because he couldn't do it himself. I would cook and leave the food and all I asked her to do was warm it and give it to him. She said, "If I could get off the job and take this sister to the hospital then I could get off and come home and warm my husband's food."

My husband's eyes would roll up until you could hardly see the black and he would stand in place and move as if he was walking. His hands shook so bad until he could hardly hold anything. One day she shocked me by asking me to get him ready that she wanted to take him to church. I bathe him, got him dressed and went to town to get dark shades so no one could see his eyes. She was all smiles when she picked him up. I was glad that she wanted him to go with her.

Before dismissal when the pastor asked if any visitors had anything to say, my sister-in-law stood with tears running down her face and told the people, "That she had to bathe him and get him ready for church because his little wife didn't have time for him, she had to see about him." She said, "I wouldn't cook for him, didn't see about his needs and he was going blind." She stood in the church and cried like a baby, and many of the people there believed her.

One day I went to the church for a function and the pastor was talking to the people after it was over, she came and took me to him and said, "Pastor this is my little sister-in-law." He was about to shake my hand and just turned and walked away and she stood there smiling.

My sister-in-law would say to her friend in my presence, "this is my brother's little wife and she say she is saved", and just laugh. I always showed her respect never argued with her and allowed her to say whatever she wanted. The only time I was angry enough to stand up to her, my husband and I was having a heated argument that was loud and she heard us and came to the house. I turned on her and was angry enough to fight her. After only a few words, it felt like all the air went out of me because I remembered this woman is as old as my mother. I immediately hushed and allowed her to talk against me.

Her daughter-in-law, Ann told me I should have kept telling her off and if she didn't hush, I should have cursed her out because that's what she would have done. But my mother's teaching was so deeply imbedded in me that I could never disrespect her even though she disrespected me.

Again, I had to contend with my husband, his sister and brother on one side and Apostle on the other.

CHAPTER FOURTEEN

In the year 1980, my sister-in-law became sick and even though I lived talking distance from her I didn't know she was sick. She had turned her children against me so they didn't bother to tell me she was sick. I knew that I hadn't seen her for a while but I was trying to avoid her anyways. My sister-in-law died from that sickness.

Apostle continued to tell me that he loved me and praised my name before our leader and the Albany church, but little did they know how bad I was treated in Newton. He always told us if we took him to the leader, he would come out on top, and we believed him.

One day he rebuked me in front of the church and told me he didn't want me to do anything else for him. He was angry at me because of the Sunday School books. He said that he wanted another young lady in the church to take charge and I had better not touch it. I took him at his word and intentionally didn't bother even though I knew this young lady hadn't done what she was told.

Our books at that time were ordered through our head-quarter church and when out leader called for a minister

In The Name of Love

council all ministers from ever church had to attend. In the council, all business was discussed. I had always made sure that all his church business was taken care of and his name wasn't called for anything, at this council meeting, his name was called and he jumped up, looked at me and said my name. I had to stand and give an answer as to why his Sunday School's order hadn't been made.

I stood and told the leader that Apostle said that he didn't want me to see about anything for him that this other sister would see about the books.

The Apostle standing said, calling the leader's name over and over, "I did this, you see this minister tries to see about everything in the church. She does the work of the deacon; the secretary and I was only trying to take some of the load off her."

The leader rebuked me and said, "You think you are something, you hide behind this Apostle, but I can pull you away from Newton and really give you something to do. You better never let this happen again." This convinced me even more that if we went against the Apostle, we would lose.

Chapter Fifteen

My husband stopped taking his medication and his eyes came back to normal and he started treating me worse. He would curse me until I went to bed at night calling me every bad name he could think of. I went to sleep with him standing over the bed cursing me and when I wake the next morning, he would still be cursing me. I wandered did he even go to sleep because I would still be in bed and that's how he woke me in the mornings.

Nothing stopped me from being faithful to God, my leader, my pastor and my church.

One Sunday in Albany our leader was taking the church with him to Albany State College, for night service. He was speaking at Caroline Hall.

During that time, we were forbidden to eat anywhere but the church because we had cooks in the kitchen that prepared food for everyone.

When me and two of the sisters made it to the kitchen, they had sold out and there was no more food. We hadn't eaten all day and were very hungry. The two sisters went to the Apostle and was talking with him. I went up and joined them. They were telling the Apostle that they were going to get something to eat, because they weren't going to the Hall hungry, and there wasn't any food in the kitchen.

He laughed with them and didn't tell them that they couldn't go and buy food. I was the one driving so when he didn't object, I took them. They bought their food, but I was afraid to buy anything so I continued to go hungry. I wouldn't even take any of their food when they offered to share with me. I was just that afraid of getting in trouble.

When we got to Caroline Hall, the Apostle was waiting on the outside. Usually, he would have been with the leader, because he was the leader's right hand's man. He stood beside my car and watched them eat, laughing and talking with them. I still wouldn't eat anything and he know it because one of the sisters (the one he called his baby) said I was crazy for not eating.

At that time, we stayed in the church late, but after coming home and going to bed, Apostle came to my house. He pulled up to my bedroom window with the lights shining bright through an he was screaming my name, saying get up, get up now. I jumped up threw on a robe and went to the door. He came in screaming at me because the two sisters had bought food. The more I tried to explain that they had talked to him the more he screamed and threaten me. He said I'm going to report you to the leader and have him take your minister license if it's the last thing I do. It was about three o'clock in the morning, and my husband had come into the room. The more Apostle screamed and fussed at me, the more my husband laughed. All I could do was stand there in my night clothes and cry.

Even after the Apostle left my husband still laughed. He thought it funny and seem to get pleasure out of the situation. He loved to see me hurt by the church people.

CHAPTER SIXTEEN

Everywhere the Apostle went that didn't require staying overnight, me and the sister he called his baby went. Regardless of what he did we loved him and would follow him anywhere. He would talk to us about things that he didn't want his wife to know. We had this weird relationship with him. I say weird because no matter how he hurt us, we followed behind him like little sheep, and there was nothing we wouldn't talk to him about.

Our lives were an open book to him. We talked to him about intimate subjects, our husbands and everything else. We loved following him.

I only worked parttime on my job. I went to work anytime I wanted to. I hardly ever got to work before 10 o'clock but the work day started at 7:30am. My boss knew the problems I had at home with my husband and he let me by with just about anything. Everyone in Newton know about my husband and the problems or sickness that he suffered from. No matter what time I went to work, I worked hard and turned out as much work as some of those that has worked all day. My job was about speed and I worked very fast.

Sometimes the Apostle wanted me to follow him and my boss objected but I would leave anyway. My boss also knew the Apostle and his reputation as a pastor. My boss would be cursing and saying he needed me to work, but I would gather my belonging and walk out. I never got fired but showed up the next day as if nothing had happened.

God was so good to me. Sometime when my boss wanted to get something over to the line that I worked on or other ladies, he would walk up behind me, scream my name and start fussing and cursing. The whole line would go silent and sometime other lines as he told me what he expected from all of us. That was alright with me because I got away with bloody murder on that job and my boss protected me when my husband went out and charged things and put my name on the papers with his. They would try to garnishing my check but my boss would tell me not to worry about it, because he wasn't going to allow them to do so. You have to understand this was back in the 70's and 80's when the whites were getting by with anything they wanted, even trying to make me pay for things I had no idea my husband had purchased. My boss said, "they had to know something was wrong with him before they let him had whatever he had credited."

All of the men that came through my life would say they loved me. My dad, because he was my dad. The Apostle would tell me he loved me that I was a true sister.

My husband would be cursing me and calling me all kind of bad names then stop and say as if he were talking to someone else, "I love my wife, but she just don't know it." Then he would start back cursing me. My husband did that a lot almost daily saying, "I love my wife, but she just don't know it."

I learned to just walk on with my head up to let them say and do as they please. It was a very hurtful time in my life, but my leader had this pet saying, "If you can take it, you can make it."

I had learned to cry in secret because all of the hurt that the Apostle was putting me through was having an ill effect on my daughter. She loved me and was getting to despise the Apostle for the way he treated me. It seemed as if the enemy was trying to destroy me through my pastor, but at the time all I knew was that I had to obey and it was wrong to talk against him or go against him.

There was one occasion when the Apostle accused my son of something and my son denied it. Apostle grabbed him threw him down on the floor and was on top of him choking him. I was in the lady's restroom listening when I heard the thump as my son hit the floor. I ran to the office and there he was straddled my son with his hands around his throat.

The chairman deacon told me that he had told the Apostle that what my son was accused of was impossible because my son was with him, but the Apostle wouldn't listen. He began trying to hurt my son in any way he could. My son was about sixteen at the time.

I would beg my son, "just don't say anything." But he said, "I can be with a group of boys and when I see him coming, I try to hide behind them, but he will always come through them straight to me and start fussing at me for no reason.

My son had the opportunity to go to college on a scholarship as a track star and basketball player. Because of the policy of the church at that time, it forbade them from getting into school activities that would keep them away from church.

My son's gym teacher called the leader and asked him could my son participate. He explained to the leader that my son was an exceptional runner and basketball player. Our leader told the gym teacher yes that he could participate. When the Apostle found out that the leader had given his permission for my son to go with the team, he went to the leader and told him that my son didn't need to be on the team, that all the boys on the team did was take drugs, they were all drug addicts. Of course, our leader pulled him off the team and said he couldn't participate.

Some of the members said, don't let him get away with this, you know this is not true. I knew that Apostle would only accuse me of taking up for my son in his wrong to the leader because he had accused me of that very thing on another occasion when I tried to talk to him.

Apostle pressured my son until he finally left the church. In some ways, I was relieved because I was afraid all the time of Apostle pushing my son and that one day, he would stand up to him and fight. I knew the kind of man the Apostle was that it would be a fight if my son wouldn't back down. I wanted my son to be happy and I knew that he wasn't happy in the church. I wanted him to have the opportunity to live his life. He served as a guitar player in the church, but the Apostle and his wife said, we don't want him playing for us. My son blamed me until the day he died that he didn't get the chance to go to college on the scholarship. I know now that I should have protected him from the Apostle, but we were taught that going against leadership was the same as going against God, because that's who he represented. I didn't have any problem protecting him from others, because my children were the one thing that I would literally fight for and if pushed kill for, but all parents feel that way about their children. Only against the Apostle would I not defend him.

Chapter Seventeen

My son finally left home and moved to Ft. Myers Florida. He got involved with a woman there that had six children. At some point he tried to back out of the relationship but she was determined to keep him in her life. One night at about one o'clock in the morning I got a call that my son was dead. This lady went to where he was staying and stabbed him. No one can understand how much I loved my son. He was the child that I had had since I was fourteen years old.

He and my daughter were my sun, moon and stars. I loved them more than life itself. I would have gladly given my life for him and thought nothing of it.

I was numb at first, and was able to call his birth mom who was and is my sister and other members of my immediate family with the help of my daughter. He died the year she was to graduate high school.

About a month or so earlier, God had showed me in a dream my son's death. I saw a lady stab him, I saw myself going to Ft. Myers, I saw him in a refrigerator wrapped. In my dreams he was wrapped in newspapers.

I had called him and told him the dream. He told me that he would be coming home on the fourth of July 1984. Then on July 1, 1984, I got the call that my son was dead.

My niece, Ann that had been my friend when my husband sister was alive was right there. She took over and began to make arrangements for me to go to Ft. Myers to claim his body. My sister Edrena was with me also to help care for me and my daughter.

When reality hit me that my baby was really dead, I began to scream uncontrollable. I couldn't stop screaming. Matter of fact it took me two years to stop screaming. At odd moments, I would just start screaming and couldn't stop. During this time, I was still going to church still during what was expected of me, but the minute that I was alone I would start screaming.

My friend Edrena was always trying to help me because she was the only one that know what I was really going through. When I started to make arrangements for my son funeral amidst all of the screaming, the Apostle blocked me on every turn. Apostle agreed to preach the funeral, but his death came up in one of our big meetings. He said the only way he would preach the funeral it would have to be after the minister council at four in the evening and I agreed. When I began to go forth to get the program from the church, he blocked that also.

My son grew up in the church and the majority of his friends were in the church. I wanted Apostle's son to sing my son's favorite song, but he said maybe then added, "just don't put nothing on the program, leave it blank."

Amidst all the pain and the suffering that I was going through the Apostle still wouldn't really help me, or allow me to get any one from the church on the program. I finally went to the older people in the church. I called a deacon from Atlanta, got an older pastor and the husband of the old mother who had helped fed me and my children when we were in need. My older sister Joyce found a lady to sing a solo.

Our big meeting was still going on during this time for it lasted two weeks, night and day. I buried my son on the first Saturday of the conference and the next week was expected to be back in church as I did.

Standing in the church with all of the music, shouting and dancing, I didn't feel anything but the pain in my heart. I had made God a promise early when I began to take on responsibility in the church as Assistant Pastor. I promised God, I'll take care of your children and you take care of mine. The enemy was fighting me greatly because I felt God had let me down. I felt that I had kept my promise to him in seeing about his people and he had let my son die.

I stood in the services with a heavy heart. I clapped my hands because I knew it was expected of me. The leader noticed me from the pulpit that I wasn't dancing and shouting like the other members and said, "some of you are just standing there and not praising God. Just because someone has died in your family and you are going through is no reason not to give God praise." It felt as if he had stabbed me in my heart that was already hurting. I expected him to at least understand where I was and that I was suffering heartache.

I endured the rest of the services. But on my way home I could only scream and cry. I thank God for my sister Edrena because she was there trying to comfort me. She had to listen to all my screaming and crying and telling me, "It is going to be alright."

My leader didn't know how hard a time I had trying to get someone to be on program for my son's funeral and had trusted the Apostle to take care of it. When he found out he was very upset, and said I had stood with the ministry faithfully all these years and there was no way that I should have had any problems with the program that someone else in the church should have been responsible for doing it and take the burden off me.

He was upset and he let the Apostle know it. I felt better after hearing him say this.

CHAPTER EIGHTEEN

A t the church in Newton, things continued to function as usual. Apostle was a great speaker and the services were great. He had an anointing upon his life and people were continually being saved.

There was a young lady in the church that was the wife of one of our head Deacons. She was a trouble maker. One day this young lady was in the restroom crying and some of the ladies came and got me. I went and tried to console her, but she just cried. I asked who had hurt her and she said "what if it's someone high up." I told her it didn't matter if someone had wronged her to tell the Apostle. Little did I know the young lady was talking about me. She went into the office and told the Apostle and he called me in. I sat there amazed at what this lady was saying. In the middle of her talking, Apostle stopped her, looked at me and said, "I'm telling you right now minister; I believe her." Then she began to lay it on thick. After she finished her lie, then Apostle turned to me and said, "what do you have to say." I replied, "you already said you believe her so I don't have anything to say."

He got angry at me and said that I had disrespected him because I wouldn't say anything in my defense.

If I wrote all the things Apostle did to me and the young people in Newton, I would run out of ink and pen. When he took young people with him on trips, or taking them home from or to church, he would make them get on their knees in the back seat of his car, he said he was putting them on the alter. If he was angry with them, he would slap them. One young girl he would bump her head on the walls of his office.

I can't say he was prejudice, because I saw him slap his own daughter down for not walking fast enough when we called for choir practice. I had seen men slap ladies down in movies, but I didn't know it was possible for someone to slap another that hard. But he literally slapped her hard enough that her feet came off the floor. One night during a revival in Albany, his daughter and his niece was standing in service clapping their hands like everyone else. He came in walked over to them slapped his daughter, then slapped his niece. The church was full and most of the church saw him. Someone told the leader about him slapping them and the leader said it was degrading and a dishonor to slap those young people in their face and forbid him to do it ever again.

One night in revival my husband came, stepped up and said to the Apostle that he wanted to try living holy. I was shocked. I had no idea he would do this after fighting me for all those years. But when Apostle asked him are you sure this is what you want, my husband said yes. The entire church began to rejoice because they knew my husband and how he treated me. They knew how hard of a time I was having with him.

The very next day the Apostle stopped by my house to see what my husband was doing. He chewed tobacco and didn't try to hide the fact from Apostle. The Apostle only looked at him, but when he left, he called me and said, "if your husband (only he called his name) chews tobacco I am going to put him on the alter. I tried talking to Apostle and begging him, please don't bother him right now, give him a chance to stop, he doesn't have the Holy Ghost yet. Apostle got angry with me and said, "I was just taking up for my husband and he would report me." That same week he came back to my house and told my husband if he chewed any more tobacco, he was going to put him on the alter. My husband had been to church enough to know what that entailed and said I'm not getting on my knees with my *** in the air like sister W. This sister was kept on the alter a lot for any and every reason. Apostle would insist we come to church no matter what, even when we had death in our own family, if we were sick or anything else. Sister W was the only one that had the courage, when he insisted that we come sick to ask him where was his wife. He would say she wasn't feeling well or she wasn't up to coming. Sister W would say to him, we had to come anyway and some of us are sick. That always earned her the alter. She always opened her mouth about something that kept her on the alter. But of course, she only said what some of us was thinking.

My husband never came back.

Chapter Nineteen

T he Apostle left the church, his wife also in May 1987, and I became pastor of the church, July 18, 1987.

Now the church was my responsibility alone and I felt unworthy. I had been beat down my entire life and had a problem with low self-esteem. I became determined to be the best pastor that I could be and vowed always to treat people the way that I wanted to be treated.

My carnal life continued to follow the same course. My husband cursing me every day but now he seems to get worse. He took on where his sister had left off. He started telling people that I wouldn't cook for him, sleep with him or see about him. I asked him once, why do you tell people these things about me and you know they are not true. He laughed and said, "because people will give me money and buy me beer when I tell them these things."

One night I was to preach at the Americus church and my husband said I'm going. I really didn't want him to go because I didn't know what he would do. My sister Edrena and my sister Louvenia went with me also. He surprised me and acted good and I breathed a sigh of relief. On the way home he said that he wanted chips and a drink. I drove around until I found an outside vendor. My sister Edrena and I got out to get what he wanted. When we got out of the car he said to sister Louvenia, "watch this." When I got back in the car he said, "what took you so *** long, I'm hungry and you are slowing around taking your ******* time." I'm trying to explain that I just went up to the vendor and you saw us, but he cursed and screamed, raring back in the seat with his jerking. We went down the road with the car bumping.

Sister Louvenia got upset with him and told me "Pastor, I will help him whenever I can, I will help you see about him, but I will never talk to him as long as he treats you like that, because he knows what he is doing." She didn't talk to him ever again. She would see him on the streets, bring him home, give him a dollar or two if he asked her, take Sister Edrena to look for him when he didn't come home for long periods of time, but she never spoke to him. One day she saw him drunk lying beside the highway in some tall grass. She stopped picked him up, but wouldn't hold him a conversation.

Sister Edrena went looking for him many times, but I wouldn't go because he would show out on me. Sister Edrena would find him along with Sister Louvenia and start beating him until he came home. He would just laugh at her, but no one else could do that to him.

My husband would cheat with me standing there. He would go out have sex with other women, come back and tell me what he did. Even though it hurt, I would tell him, "I can see you humping on the floor with a woman, step over your back and keep on going." I had to take this attitude to keep my husband from destroying me.

My biological sister's husband despised him, because he said it was a disrespect to me that my husband didn't care what he did in front of me. I only looked at my husband and kept going. Sometime I wanted to laugh when people would see and hear what he was doing and know that I saw him too and they would ask, "is that your husband and I would just say yes." I knew to confront him would just make everything worse.

My life seemed to deteriorate. But ever since the year 1975 when the leader prayed for me and whatever I was carrying fell off me. I was able to take all that life or better yet the enemy threw at me. But once again it was getting heavy.

My husband continued cursing me, only now he had added more hurtful things. He would scream and tell me I was no good and that he didn't want me anyway that some other man could have me. He screamed and told me this all the time. He would still say, "I love my wife, but she just don't know it."

Also, when I would go to town there was a whiskey store where lots of men hung out. Passing the store, I could hear him screaming my name cursing me, calling me every mother-so and so and no good son of a bitch he could think of.

One day I had to go to the bank and didn't get out before he got there. He came in the bank cursing me and calling me out of my name. The people in the bank would start trying to get him out and he would start crying telling the people that I was taking all his money. Other times when I went to the grocery store, he came in with the same thing cursing to the top of his voice and when the people would try and get him out, telling him he couldn't do that in the store, he would start crying, saying the same thing that I was taking all his money.

One day God visited me in a dream and said, "Hold on it will all be over in a little while." I began to rejoice. I told my sister Edrena that God said for me to hold on that this will be over in a little while. I don't know who was happier me or her. I was there for the good, bad and ugly in her life and she was there for me. I knew that I could count on her and sister Louvenia for anything, they stuck with me through thick and thin.

All I could think about was in a little while it would be over. To me a little while is a few weeks but 6 months passed. I had no thought of giving up because God had become my life. But when my suffering and going through with my husband continued and nothing got better only worse, I said, "alright God you said in a little while." Then a year passed, and that little while began to look a little dimmer. My sister Edrena encouraged my saying, "Overseer you've just got to believe God, He promised and He is going to do it." With her help and encouragement, I kept on believing God.

CHAPTER TWENTY

Two years later my husband came home after being with his buddies all day. His sister that lived in Canton, Ohio was the one in charge of distributing the money from the farm. When he came home, I was getting ready for church, we were in one of our big conferences. He asked me, "did you go to the mailbox today, and I said no. He said I'm going to the mailbox to see if my check has come. She was supposed to have mailed it weeks ago and hadn't.

When he didn't come back in the house to eat, I said, "I guess some of his friends has picked him up and he's gone back to town." I finished getting ready and went to the door to leave and saw all these police cars with their lights blinking. I watched them from the door. Instead of leaving for church as I planned, I walked out to the highway and watched the police shining their flash lights walking from the mailbox to a distance up the road.

After I continued standing there for some time, a young man that I had known since I came to Newton, came to me and said, "Pastor he is gone." A car had hit him crossing the highway. The young lady that hit him was a longtime family friend, and I pastored about fifteen members of her family. My husband died in 1994.

Chapter Twenty-One

I never knew why God allowed me to go through so much, but I would like to think that I went through so that I would be able to help His people. That I can encourage the young person that's going through abuse at home, the wife or husband that has In-law problems, or the wife that has a cheating, or abusive husband or the person who has an abusive Pastor. I do know that God has a plan and purpose for everything that I suffered and went through.

I can testify that God is a keeper and if you put your trust in him, he'll bring you through everything that the enemy puts you through, and we can be more that a conqueror through Christ Jesus.

No matter what I was going through in my home, God kept raising me higher in the ministry. In 1987, I became a Pastor; June 1991, I became an Overseer, and three years later, September 1994, I became Head Overseer of Evangelical Faith Vision Ministry. Today, I now preside as the First Lady Bishop of Evangelical Faith Vision Ministry.

I thank God for His Grace and Mercy!

FINAL WORDS

Throughout my journey from childhood to adulthood, God has shown me He was there all the time. Many things that happen in our lives, the Devil mean it for evil, but God will make it for our good. For everything we go through, there is a purpose and a plan for our lives.

Therefore, this book was not written to condemn, judge or attack anyone's character, it was mainly written to encourage the ones that no matter the situation or think they can't make it or that suicide may be the answer. I hope this book will help anyone to discover the power of God that what you are going through is not the end.

When you are faithful to God, He will be faithful to you!

ABOUT THE AUTHOR

Gladis Jones Hall is the presiding Pastor of Circle of Love Restoration Temple and First Moultrie Holiness Deliverance Church. She grew up in the small town of Colquitt, GA and graduated from Bethel High School. She married the late Bynes Hall and moved to Newton, GA, where she accepted Christ as her Lord and Savior. She then began inspiring others to come to Christ and served in ministry for over fifty years. She was born June 12, 1943 in Colquitt, Ga and is the sixth child of seven siblings. She has two children, Ms. Sharon Miller and the late Ronald Jones. To her collections of children, she raised her grandson, Latavius Montgomery Jones and a bonus son Johnny Jackson. Currently, she has five grand-children and several great grands that she greatly loves and cherishes.

CPSIA information can be obtained
at www.ICGtesting.com
Printed in the USA
BVHW071914130223
658422BV00012B/152

9 781662 869471